SPECIAL LIVES IN HISTORY THAT BECOME

Signature LIVES

HARRIET BEECHER
STOWE
AUTHOR AND ADVOCATE

by Brenda Haugen

Content Adviser: Dawn C. Adiletta, Curator,
Harriet Beecher Stowe Center,
Hartford, Connecticut

Reading Adviser: Rosemary G. Palmer, Ph.D.,
Department of Literacy, College of Education,
Boise State University

COMPASS POINT BOOKS MINNEAPOLIS, MINNESOTA

Compass Point Books
3109 West 50th Street, #115
Minneapolis, MN 55410

Visit Compass Point Books on the Internet at *www.compasspointbooks.com*
or e-mail your request to *custserv@compasspointbooks.com*

Managing Editor: Catherine Neitge
Lead Designer: Jaime Martens
Photo Researcher: Marcie C. Spence
Cartographer: XNR Productions, Inc.
Educational Consultant: Diane Smolinski

Art Director: Keith Griffin
Production Director: Keith McCormick
Creative Director: Terri Foley

To all the teachers in Wyndmere who encouraged me to write
and gave me the freedom to go beyond the "recommended reading list."
I've never forgotten. BLH

Library of Congress Cataloging-in-Publication Data
Haugen, Brenda.
  Harriet Beecher Stowe : author and advocate / by Brenda Haugen.
    p. cm. — (Signature lives)
  Includes bibliographical references and index.
  ISBN 0-7565-0822-3 (hardcover)
  1. Stowe, Harriet Beecher, 1811–1896—Juvenile literature. 2. United
States—History—Civil War, 1861–1865—Literature and the war—Juvenile
literature. 3. Authors, American—19th century—Biography—Juvenile
literature. 4. Abolitionists—United States—Biography—Juvenile literature.
I. Title. II. Series.
  PS2956.H38 2005
  813'.3—dc22   2004018755

CIVIL WAR ERA

The Civil War (1861-1865) split the United States into two countries and divided the people over the issue of slavery. The opposing sides—the Union in the North and the Confederacy in the South—battled each other for four long years in the deadliest American conflict ever fought. The bloody war sometimes pitted family members and friends against each other over the issues of slavery and states' rights. Some of the people who lived and served their country during the Civil War are among the nation's most beloved heroes.

Table of Contents

1 FIGHTING INJUSTICE

⚬ᘰᕽᘰᘰ

Harriet Beecher Stowe couldn't sleep. For more than a year, she had been consumed with grief after the death of her infant son Charley. Now in September 1850, more sadness entered her life, and she felt just as helpless to do anything about it.

Stowe was angered and saddened by the Compromise of 1850. Championed by politicians Daniel Webster, Stephen Douglas, and Henry Clay, the compromise was supposed to ease tension between slaveholders in the South and abolitionists in the North.

The tension had increased after the Mexican War (1846–1848), when the United States gained new territory. Southern states wanted these new territories to come into the Union as slave states. The Northern states didn't want slavery to spread any farther.

Harriet Beecher Stowe became known around the world with the publication of her book Uncle Tom's Cabin.

Under the Compromise of 1850, California joined the Union as a free state. The slavery question in New Mexico and Utah was left to future settlers to decide.

What upset Stowe was one specific part of the compromise: the Fugitive Slave Act. Under this act, runaway slaves who escaped north to freedom were required to be returned to their masters in the South. Stowe, a Northerner living in Maine, hated slavery and wished she could do something to bring it to an end.

Other members of her family also hated slavery and did what they could. Her brother Henry Ward Beecher used his position as a minister to bring attention to the issue. He even encouraged his congregation to buy slaves and grant them their freedom. Harriet's brother Edward also talked to his church members about the evils of the new law and encouraged them to ignore it.

Stowe wrote passionate letters to her family members about the Fugitive Slave Act. She had

Black slaves were found in the American colonies as early as the 1600s. In 1641, Massachusetts became the first colony to declare slavery a legal institution. In 1663, a Virginia court ruled that a child born to a female slave was also a slave. The crops plantation owners grew, such as tobacco, rice, and cotton, required many hands to help tend them. Slave labor was the option many Southerners chose to get their plantation work done. By the time of the Civil War, about 4 million slaves lived in the United States. Almost one in three people living in Southern slave states at that time was a slave.

The runaway slave Scipio is hunted by a mob as his master, St. Clare, tries to save him. The engraving is from the first British edition of Uncle Tom's Cabin.

long, heated arguments with some of her neighbors on the issue. Still, she longed to do more.

For years, Stowe helped her family make ends meet by selling articles she wrote to various magazines. Her sister-in-law Isabella suggested Harriet use her gift of writing to fight the injustice of the Fugitive Slave Act.

"Now, Hattie, if I could use a pen as you can, I would write something that would make this whole

11

A poster for Uncle Tom's Cabin from the 1930s, more than 80 years after the book was published.

nation feel what an accursed thing slavery is," Isabella wrote to Harriet.

Harriet read Isabella's letter to her children and then rose to her feet.

"I will write something," Stowe declared. "I will if I live." The story Stowe wrote was titled *Uncle Tom's Cabin*. Not only would it bring atten- tion to the injustice and cruelty of slav- ery, it would further split an already divided country. President Abra- ham Lincoln would even credit Stowe with being one of the causes for the Civil War.

Harriet Beecher Stowe

The book threw this 39-year-old mother into the spotlight. Stowe became the best-known American woman in the world. She used the spotlight to spread her message of freedom, proving just how mighty the pen can be. ∿

2 GROWING UP

❧◈❧

"Hattie is a genius," Lyman Beecher said of his daughter Harriet when she was a little girl. "I would give a hundred dollars if she were a boy."

Harriet's father believed men and women were equal before God and had equal responsibilities to do good, but that was as far as it went. Men and women were not equal in the eyes of the world. Lyman expected his sons to grow up to be preachers, just like him. In those days, daughters usually either married or lived at home for the rest of their lives. The Reverend Beecher never dreamed of the impact his little girl would have on the world.

Harriet Elizabeth Beecher was born June 14, 1811, in a plain frame house in Litchfield, Connecticut. Hattie, as her friends and family called her, was the

Lyman Beecher had a habit of pushing his glasses—or spectacles, as they were called in the early 19th century —on top of his head whenever he got excited during a sermon. Forgetting the glasses were there, Beecher often pulled another pair out of one of his pockets. At the end of a really good sermon, he sometimes ended up with three pairs of glasses on the top of his head!

seventh of nine children born to Lyman and Roxanna Beecher.

Growing up, Harriet and her younger brother Henry Ward Beecher often were mistaken as twins. They were two years apart in age, and they really enjoyed each other's company. Harriet and Henry walked to school together. In the summertime, they would gather blueberries, black raspberries, strawberries, and chestnuts. In the winter months, the two often coasted down hills together on sleds.

Harriet and Henry also got into trouble together. One day, their mother made the mistake of leaving all her flower bulbs in the house—in reach of Harriet and Henry. Mrs. Beecher loved flowers. Thinking the bulbs were sweet onions, the two children devoured them as soon as their mother left the house. When their mother returned, all the bulbs were gone.

"My dear children, what you have done makes mamma very sorry," Mrs. Beecher said quietly. "Those were not onions but roots of beautiful flowers, and if you had let them alone we should have next summer in the garden great beautiful red and yellow flowers such as you never saw."

A quiet, gentle person, Roxanna Beecher did not have to yell or punish her children further. They felt sorry for what they had done because it had made their mother so sad.

Harriet enjoyed making people laugh. Sometimes she'd make silly faces to get a chuckle. She also was known as a tomboy and a hard worker. She helped pile wood to heat the family's home. She loved to fish, hike, and climb trees.

She also loved her parents. While her mother was shy, reserved, and very smart, her father was powerful and quick to share his strong opinions. One of the most famous preachers of his time, Lyman Beecher was strict with his children. If they squirmed around during his Sunday church sermons, they would go to bed without dinner that evening.

Lyman Beecher

However, Harriet's father also found time to have fun. He took his sons hunting and fishing. The entire family went on picnics and hayrides.

The Reverend Beecher also believed exercise was very important. He kept a pile of sand in the cellar and shoveled it from one corner of the room to the other if the weather kept him from going outside for exercise.

The Beecher family posed for a photo in 1850. Standing from left: Thomas, William, Edward, Charles, and Henry; seated from left: Isabella, Catharine, Lyman, Mary, and Harriet; inset: James.

He also taught all of his children to appreciate music. The Beechers held family "sings," with older sisters Catharine and Mary playing the piano. Brothers Edward and William joined in on flute, while their father played the violin, though not very well.

"So we had often domestic concerts, which, if

they did not attain to the height of artistic perfection, filled the house with gladness," Harriet remembered.

Their lives were soon touched with sorrow, though. In 1816, Mrs. Beecher died of tuberculosis. Harriet's 16-year-old sister Catharine stepped in to help raise Harriet, who was only 5 years old at the time, and their siblings. Their father would later remarry and have four more children, but Catharine would serve as more of a mother to Harriet than her stepmother would.

Harriet struggled to move past her mother's death. As she often did in her childhood, she went to spend time at her grandmother's farm, named Nutplains. Harriet went with her aunt Harriet Foote to Grandmother Foote's farm just outside Guilford, Connecticut.

Tuberculosis is an infectious disease that mainly affects a person's lungs. It was once known as consumption because its victims would waste away if they did not receive treatment. The disease is caused by bacteria and prior to the late 1800s, it ranked as one of the most common causes of death throughout the world. Modern medicine can treat tuberculosis effectively today, but in undeveloped countries and among the world's poor, tuberculosis still claims many lives. Tuberculosis is the main cause of death worldwide in people infected with HIV.

At Grandmother Foote's home, Harriet met Dinah and Harry, African-Americans who were probably former slaves. Lyman had taught Harriet that all people are equal, but Aunt Harriet bossed

Catharine Beecher in 1848

Dinah and Harry around and didn't treat them as well as she treated white people. Even at such a young age, Harriet knew that was wrong, and she wouldn't forget it.

At 5 years old, Harriet was ready to go to school. Right from the start, she was a good student and loved school.

"Hattie is a very good girl," Catharine wrote in November 1816. "She has been to school all this summer, and has learned to read very fluently."

By the time Harriet was 6, she was borrowing books from her father's library. While the Reverend Beecher didn't earn much money, he did collect hundreds of books. He gladly shared them with Harriet. Often she'd sit in the corner of his library and read while he wrote his sermon for the week.

She enjoyed reading history books, including Cotton Mather's history of New England that featured tales about Indian culture and witchcraft. Lyman didn't really believe Harriet understood what she was reading, but before she turned 8 years old,

Harriet convinced him that she did.

Harriet entered Litchfield Academy in 1819 at age 8. Most students didn't start until they were at least 12. She quickly became the top student in her class. One of Harriet's proudest moments would come about two years later. She was one of several academy students selected to write an essay. When her essay was read at graduation, Harriet was thrilled to see the look of pride on her father's face. She would continue to write for the rest of her life. ❧

Chapter

3 Teacher, Writer, and Mother

⁓⟡⁓

In the spring of 1823, Catharine and Mary Beecher, Harriet's elder sisters, founded a school for girls in Hartford, Connecticut. Harriet enrolled in Catharine's Hartford Female Seminary the following September as one of its first students. By the time she turned 16, Harriet was not only continuing her own education, but also teaching other students there, since Mary had given up teaching when she got married.

Studying Italian, Latin, French, and philosophy, Harriet also enjoyed reading the romantic poetry of Lord Byron. Harriet dreamed of becoming a poet, but Catharine thought she should spend her time teaching instead. Harriet continued to write, hiding her poetry from her sister. Harriet would write late at night by candlelight or a whale oil lamp, a habit

Chained slaves walk past the unfinished Capitol building in Washington, D.C., in 1820.

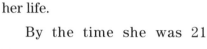

Catharine's fiancé, Alexander Fisher, died in a shipwreck off the coast of Ireland in the early 1820s. He left her $2,000, which was quite a bit of money for that time. She used it to open her school. Catharine never married.

she would continue throughout her life.

By the time she was 21, Harriet was teaching full time at Catharine's school. She loved art and was able to share that with students in her drawing and painting classes.

In 1832, the Beecher family moved to Cincinnati, Ohio. Lyman Beecher had been named the first president of Lane Theological Seminary. Nine of the Beechers, Harriet included, piled their luggage into a series of stagecoaches and canal boats and headed west. Catharine chose to move with the family and open another school—the Western Female Institute—in Cincinnati. Harriet would continue to work with her sister at the new school.

Harriet worked long hours. She got up at 6 A.M. to be at the institute by 7. She frequently stayed at the school until late at night to make sure all her work was done. She didn't get paid anything extra for working such long hours. The institute had a tight budget. Often the school couldn't buy enough textbooks for its students. To help out, Harriet wrote a geography book, which the school would use for many years.

In fact, Harriet would much rather write than

teach. The success of her geography book—she was paid $187 for it, almost as much as Catharine earned in a year—encouraged her to start her next work, *New England Sketches*.

Catharine didn't really like to teach either. She liked to organize the schools, establish the curriculum, and then get others to teach. Harriet's lack of desire to teach, and Catharine's pressure on her to work long hours were sources of irritation between the two women.

The Beecher house in Cincinnati was called Walnut Hills.

Though she worked hard, Harriet did find time to have some fun and meet new friends. Her uncle Samuel Foote made sure of it.

Uncle Samuel also lived in Cincinnati and had been a regular part of Harriet's childhood in Litchfield. A world traveler, he had brought the Beecher children gifts from faraway places, including Turkey and the North African country of Morocco.

Slave labor kept the Southern cotton industry booming.

Samuel also talked Harriet into joining the Semi-Colon Club. The club met each Monday, often at

Samuel's home, to talk about books and to socialize. The club was a mix of seriousness and fun. It also was a chance for members to read their personal writings to one another. At each meeting, a member was chosen to read the week's contributions. The articles could be signed by the author or the author could remain secret.

Salmon P. Chase became a U.S. senator, secretary of the treasury, and eventually chief justice of the Supreme Court. He and Harriet remained friends throughout their lives.

The Semi-Colon Club included professional authors, lawyers, and many other important community people. Judge James Hall, a member of the Semi-Colon Club and the editor of *Western Monthly Magazine*, particularly enjoyed Harriet's work. He encouraged her to continue writing and ended up publishing her first story. Hall also encouraged Harriet to send in a short story to a writing competition that his magazine was sponsoring. When Harriet won, she received a prize of $50, which was a lot of money in 1834.

Harriet also met Salmon P. Chase through the Semi-Colon Club. A young lawyer, Chase was active in the antislavery movement. How the slaveholding system worked in the South was a topic of much discussion.

Beginning in the early 1800s, the South had gone through a cotton boom. People grew rich as cotton prices rose. However, cotton wore out the soil quickly. Growers pushed west into Georgia and Alabama in search of richer soil and took their slaves with them, spreading slavery farther.

In the 1700s, there had been talk of slavery ending. Keeping slaves wasn't cheap, and most people knew slavery was wrong. That talk died down, though, when Eli Whitney invented the cotton gin in 1793. This new invention made separating cottonseeds from the cotton fibers faster and easier. No longer would people have to spend long hours cleaning the cotton by hand. They could now plant much more cotton and continue using slave laborers to do the work.

Another invention also helped bring on the cotton boom. A spindle was created that made it possible to spin a fine cotton thread quickly. With this new spindle and the cotton gin, cotton became widely used as a fabric that people could afford. Again, more cotton was needed, and more slaves were used to care for it. People were getting rich raising and selling cotton.

As talk of slavery dominated the conversation of the Semi-Colon Club, two people joined the group who would become very important in Harriet's life— Calvin and Eliza Stowe. The Reverend Beecher had hired Calvin as Lane Theological Seminary's first professor. Calvin Stowe would be the only professor the seminary would have for some time.

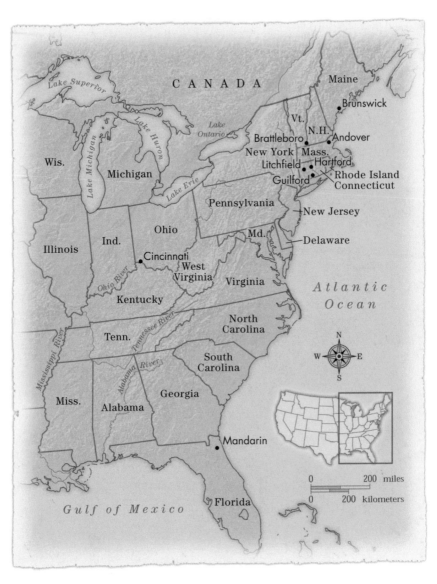

Harriet Beecher and Eliza Stowe quickly became best friends. Their friendship would not last long, though. Tiny and fragile, Eliza became ill with cholera and died unexpectedly in 1834.

Harriet Beecher Stowe lived in the East, Ohio, and Florida.

29

The Stowe family lived in Cincinnati, Ohio, for nearly 15 years.

The Beecher family watched out for Calvin after Eliza's death. He often was invited to the Beecher home for meals—for in his grief, he would forget to eat. Harriet helped Calvin by doing things he would forget about in his absentmindedness. She would mend his clothes and even fix his broken glasses. The great sadness they felt over Eliza's death brought Harriet and Calvin closer together. In time, they fell in love and were married on January 6, 1836.

Harriet loved Calvin's sense of humor. She also admired how smart he was. Calvin could speak Italian, German, Latin, Hebrew, Greek, Arabic, Spanish, and French. He was an expert in the field of education, and he knew the Bible even better than Harriet's father.

However, Calvin Stowe was forgetful and fussy. He counted on Harriet to keep him organized. That was a major mistake on his part because Harriet was notoriously disorganized. He wasn't good in a crisis either. In times of stress, Calvin often just went to bed and stayed there. Harriet became the one to handle most of the difficulties that they faced in their lives.

> *Calvin Stowe thought he saw phantoms throughout his whole life. He said the mysterious figures sometimes came out of furniture or up from the floor. No one in the Beecher family seemed to think that was strange. They believed him. They also believed Calvin was psychic. He frequently sensed events before they happened.*

Life often was a struggle for the Stowes. Harriet and Calvin would have seven children, and their problems grew along with their family. They could barely survive on Calvin's small salary. Sometimes they had to get by on even less. The seminary was just getting started, and many times Calvin could only be paid a fraction of his wages.

Harriet cooked, cleaned, mended clothing, shopped for groceries, and cared for her children and husband. Even with a large family, Harriet continued to find time to write. She needed the money. In a letter to a friend, she wrote: "If you see my name coming out everywhere—you may be sure of one thing, that I *do* it for the *pay*."

the summer of 1845, an already tired Stowe became gravely ill. Doctors could do nothing for her, and it appeared as though she would die.

Harriet clung to life as her husband, her father, and her brothers prayed over her bed. She slowly began to recover, but by early 1846, it seemed as though she might be an invalid the rest of her life. But her sister Catharine stepped in and insisted

Henry Ward Beecher (left) and his father, Lyman, prayed for Harriet's recovery.

Harriet go to a health spa in Brattleboro, Vermont, and be under a doctor's care. Friends and admirers of the Stowe family agreed to pay the expense. Harriet stayed in Vermont for a year and wrote to Calvin when her strength began to return.

> *For this week, I have gone before breakfast to the wave-bath and let all the waves and billows roll over me till every limb ached with cold and my hands would scarcely have feeling enough to dress me. After that I have walked till I was warm, and come home to breakfast with such an appetite! Brown bread and milk are luxuries indeed, and the only fear is that I may eat too much.*

When Harriet returned home, she told Calvin the doctor's treatment would be good for him, too. Calvin agreed. He left for Brattleboro in June 1848, but he wasn't going to stay as long as Harriet did. While he wasn't working, Calvin wouldn't be paid. Harriet would have to pay for his treatments at the health spa. Neither Calvin nor Harriet knew it would be more than a year before they would see one another again. ❧

4 UNCLE TOM'S CABIN

෨ଈୄଈ

While Calvin was in Vermont, a new cholera epidemic hit Cincinnati. This outbreak was killing more than 100 people every day. In a letter to Calvin, Harriet wrote about the sadness all around her:

> *Hearse drivers have scarce been allowed to unharness their horses while furniture carts and common vehicles are often employed for the removal of the dead. ... On Tuesday, one hundred and sixteen deaths from cholera were reported, and that night the air was of that peculiarly oppressive, deathly kind that seems to lie like lead on the brain and soul.*

The disease didn't miss the Stowe family. When two of the children became sick in 1849, Calvin wanted to return home. Afraid Calvin would fall ill,

In the 1850s, Henry Ward Beecher's church helped lead the charge to arm people moving to Kansas who were opposed to slavery. Settlers from the North and South flocked to Kansas in an effort to affect whether the new state would allow slavery. Beecher's church sent rifles to antislavery sympathizers. The rifles were nicknamed Beecher's Bibles because they were sent in boxes that were supposed to contain Bibles. Kansas entered the Union as a free state on January 29, 1861.

too, Harriet told him to stay in Vermont. She didn't need another sick person to nurse.

The couple's infant son, Samuel Charles, seemed to be recovering from his battle with cholera when he suddenly took a turn for the worse. When Charley died in July, Stowe was heartbroken. She believed she really knew how slave mothers felt when they were separated from their children forever.

Harriet told Calvin in a letter what had happened, and he soon returned home. Not long afterward, Calvin was offered a teaching job at Bowdoin College in Brunswick, Maine. Tired of Cincinnati and their struggles there, he accepted the position.

However, he was still under contract to teach in Cincinnati. So in early 1850, Harriet and the children left for Maine without him to get settled.

Stowe decided to take her time on the journey to Maine. She stopped in Brooklyn, New York, to see her brother Henry Ward Beecher. Now a successful pastor, Beecher actively served in the antislavery movement. He raised money through his church to buy the freedom of slave children and helped the antislavery cause in any way he could.

After a few days in Brooklyn, Stowe headed to Hartford, Connecticut, to see her sisters Mary and Isabella. Then she traveled to Boston, Massachusetts, to stay a few days with her brother Edward.

From Boston, Stowe and the children took a steamer to Maine. If Stowe had hoped Maine would be a good change for her family, she quickly changed her mind. She and the children were greeted by a storm as the steamer made its way to their new home. They were grateful to arrive in Brunswick

Henry Ward Beecher offers a slave for sale to members of his congregation. They bought her freedom.

safely, but were unhappy to discover their new house was dreary and damp. Stowe, however, was determined to do the best she could to make it better. She cleaned, put up new wallpaper, and painted the wood floors.

The Stowes still hadn't escaped their money troubles. By wintertime, holes appeared in Harriet's shoes, and she couldn't afford to buy new ones. In addition, Maine experienced a record cold spell.

The Stowe house in Brunswick, Maine

During one storm, the Stowes' house grew so cold that the children had a hard time sitting still long enough to eat. Harriet and her sister Catharine, who was living with them, worked with the older daughters to try to make enough comforters to pile on top of the smaller children at night to keep them warm.

Stowe managed to keep up with her writing. She soon started working on a story that came to her when she was in church. In her mind, she saw a black man being beaten by two others as a white man urged the two to continue. The man being beaten looked at those tormenting him with pity and forgave them. Harriet rushed home to write down her story.

When she finished, Harriet read the story to her children. They wept. When Calvin later came across the pages, he sat down and read the story and had the same reaction.

"Hattie," he told his wife, "this is the climax of that story of slavery you promised sister Katey you would write. Begin at the beginning, and work up to this and you'll have your book."

Harriet's sister-in-law, Isabella Beecher, who was married to Edward, had told Harriet she should put her writing talents to good use by writing a story to help the antislavery cause. With Calvin's reminder, Stowe needed no further encouragement. She contacted the editor of an antislavery paper called the *National Era* and told him about her story. She

*From the
manuscript of*
Uncle Tom's Cabin

expected it would have three or four installments.

"It will be ready in two or three weeks," Stowe told the editor, who agreed to pay her $300 for her finished story.

Stowe got right to work. She dug back in her memory. She started writing a story that was a combination of many things that had stuck in her mind for a long time.

She thought about stories she'd heard about slavery from Eliza Buck, a black woman she knew in Cincinnati. Buck had been a slave but had escaped to the North. Buck had told Stowe stories about slaves being beaten until they were unconscious and then left in the fields to die. Other slaves risked their own lives to creep down to the fields at night to see if they could help them, Buck said.

Stowe also remembered the Underground Railroad. It was a network of safe places for slaves to stay and of people who wanted to aid them. The Underground Railroad helped thousands of slaves escape through the northern United States into

Canada from 1830 to 1860. Because it was so close to slave territory, Cincinnati had become an important station on the Underground Railroad. Stowe had known people who had worked on the Underground Railroad when she lived in Ohio.

One of those people was the Reverend John Rankin, who lived on a bluff overlooking the Ohio River. Each evening, he lit a lantern and put it in a window facing the river. The lantern light appeared

Slaves escape to freedom on the Underground Railroad.

According to family stories, Calvin Stowe and Henry Ward Beecher helped a young woman who worked for the Stowes to escape on the Underground Railroad. Slave catchers had arrived in Cincinnati looking for a runaway. The young woman, who worked as a servant in the Stowe house, confessed she was the one being sought. Stowe and Beecher hid her in a wagon and drove her to a safe house, and she escaped. Harriet also actively participated at least once. In Maine, she let a fugitive spend the night in her house.

as a twinkle from the Kentucky side of the river.

When Harriet, Calvin, and Lyman visited Rankin, they asked him why he put the lantern in the window. He explained that runaway slaves knew the light was a beacon of freedom. They could stop at his Ohio home for food and clothing before heading on to freedom in Canada.

The minister told them stories about fugitive slaves he had helped. One story detailed the escape of a mother who crossed the river on winter ice that was beginning to break away. He had given the woman and her baby dry clothes and food before helping them on to another shelter farther north.

Stowe's memories flowed onto the paper. She wrote and wrote. Finally, after months of writing—not two or three weeks as she had expected—*Uncle Tom's Cabin* was done.

The story first appeared as a serial with monthly installments in the *National Era*. Stowe was literally creating the story as it was being published. She

missed at least one deadline, forcing the *National Era* to print an apology saying the increasingly popular story would continue in the next issue.

"Today I have taken my pen from the last chapter of *Uncle Tom's Cabin* and I think you will understand me when I say that I feel as if I had written some of it almost with my heart's blood," Stowe wrote to the man who published the story.

In an illustration from Uncle Tom's Cabin, *a desperate Eliza runs across a frozen river with her son in her arms to keep him from being sold.*

Up until she began writing *Uncle Tom's Cabin,* Stowe felt little desire to get into the slavery issue. She had written a few antislavery articles before, but the Fugitive Slave Act of 1850 had set off her anger like nothing else before it.

The new law required everyone to aid in the capture of runaway slaves and imposed fines and jail sentences on those who did not. Stowe felt called upon to show the cruelty of slavery and work to bring it to an end.

"I shall show the best side of the thing and something faintly approaching the worst," she said as she began to write *Uncle Tom's Cabin.*

The *National Era* paid Stowe $300 for *Uncle Tom's Cabin,* as agreed upon. The Washington, D.C., paper ran the story as a serial beginning in June 1851 and ending in April 1852.

A few weeks before the serialized version of the story finished running, *Uncle Tom's Cabin* was published as a book. The publisher had offered Stowe half the profits from the book if she agreed to pay for half the cost of publishing it. The Stowes didn't have enough money to risk on publishing a book. A friend of the family suggested they take a 10 percent royalty on the book instead of 50 percent. In exchange for taking less of the profits, they could convince the publisher to take on all of the costs of producing the book. Stowe would make less money per book sold, but she wouldn't risk paying more for producing it than she might make in sales.

Harriet and Calvin agreed to the plan. As a married woman, Harriet was not permitted to enter a legal contract in her own name. It was ironic that the author of the most popular and successful narrative on freedom was not legally entitled to sign a contract for her own work.

Georgianna Stowe provided part of the inspiration for the character Topsey in her mother's book, Uncle Tom's Cabin.

Stowe didn't have high hopes for *Uncle Tom's Cabin*. She didn't believe it was very good and wished she could have done better. She was sure her friends would be disappointed in her and that few copies would sell. However, she did hope she'd earn enough from the book to buy a new dress.

She was in for a big surprise. Not only would the book be a huge moneymaker, but Stowe would never just be a quiet bystander on the slavery issue again. ✍

5 CONTROVERSY IN THE UNITED STATES

⌒⌒⌒⌒⌒

When the first copies of *Uncle Tom's Cabin* were printed, neither the publisher nor the Stowes could believe what was happening. Ten thousand copies of *Uncle Tom's Cabin* were snatched up by readers in the first week! Within one year, 300,000 copies of the book were sold. In time, *Uncle Tom's Cabin* would be printed around the world in about 40 different languages.

Four months after *Uncle Tom's Cabin* was published, the Stowes got the first royalty check. It was made out for $10,000! That was more money than Calvin would earn in 10 years as a professor. The book helped with the Stowes' money worries, though Stowe often found ways to spend just about all she earned.

Uncle Tom's Cabin told the story of several families,

Stowe used some of the money she earned from Uncle Tom's Cabin *to hire an artist to paint a portrait of her good friend, Eliza, Calvin's first wife. Each year on Eliza's birthday, Calvin and Harriet would sit in front of the picture and talk about all the good things they remembered about Eliza.*

but the main character was Uncle Tom, an honest, loyal, Christian slave. Stowe wanted the book to show what slavery really was like. She wanted readers to have sympathy for the black characters and realize slaves were people, too. She wanted Northerners who read the book to realize it wasn't the Southern slave owners who were bad—it was the system that was bad. She was sure that if Southerners read the book, they'd see how wrong slavery was and that it must be ended.

Uncle Tom's Cabin turned out to be the most controversial book in the history of the United States. Those who opposed slavery but wished to preserve the Union were afraid her book would bring about a civil war, even though that wasn't what Stowe intended.

In fact, she never expected reaction to her book to be as strong as it would turn out to be. She thought people in the North might be angry about her book, but not people from the South. After all, she believed she had shown Southerners in a positive way. She created more kind masters in her book than cruel ones, and Simon Legree, the worst villain

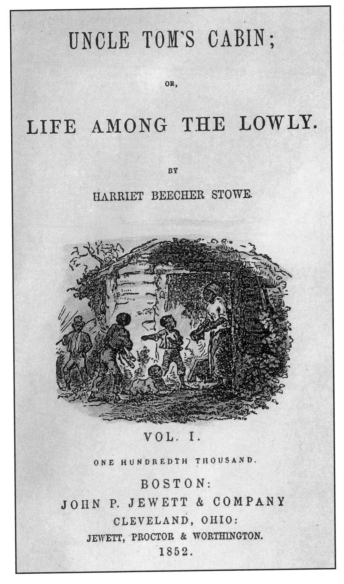

of all, was from the North. Though slavery was only legal in the South, Stowe saw it as a national problem and pointed that out in *Uncle Tom's Cabin*.

An 1850 engraving shows the cruelty of the Fugitive Slave Act.

The Southern economy depended upon slavery. Stowe believed cruelty to slaves had been going on for so long that acts of violence against slaves

weren't even seen as cruel any-more. Today's slave owners could not be blamed for that, she thought.

In Stowe's view, because Northerners bought products—such as cotton—from Southern plantation owners, they were just as much to blame for slavery's continuing existence. Northern bankers, cotton manufacturers, shippers, and others also benefited from the Southern economy and its use of slaves, Stowe pointed out.

Many churches throughout the country also should be ashamed, she said. She was angry that some churches took firm stands on minor issues—such as the stand against public dancing—but closed their eyes to the issue of slavery. Stowe believed if churches across the country stood together and said slavery should be ended, it would be. She further thought that by not taking a stand against slavery, churches were actively supporting it.

Until she wrote *Uncle Tom's Cabin*, Stowe thought the abolitionists were taking the wrong approach to the problem. She believed acts of vio-

At one point during the 1850s, 16 different groups of actors across the United States were putting on a play based on Stowe's book Uncle Tom's Cabin. The play became the most successful one of its time. Stowe never earned a penny from the performances. She had never bothered to acquire the rights to the play. In addition, the story's characters were considered to be in the public domain. So people made a fortune off the characters Stowe created.

A 19th-century engraving shows a slave trying to run away. Slaves who were at risk of escaping were forced to wear iron collars.

lence by the abolitionists would only strengthen the Southerners' stand against ending slavery. But the book didn't just galvanize Northern abolitionists, it turned Stowe into an abolitionist herself.

Stowe held strong opinions, but she actually saw herself as someone in the middle of the slavery issue. She wanted to bring Northerners and Southerners together to end slavery in a peaceful way. She was shocked when she was called a radical and a liar by people in the South after the book was published.

Southerners simply dismissed *Uncle Tom's Cabin* as untrue. They were joined by the *New York Observer*, which published an angry attack on the book. The article said it painted an untrue picture of slavery—sparking a debate in newspapers across the country. Those who felt their livelihoods were being threatened by *Uncle Tom's Cabin* said it was a book of lies. Those who were against slavery fought back and stood up for Harriet and her book. They also sent her records documenting events much like those she wrote about.

While it was a work of fiction, the book was based on fact, Stowe said. She was deeply offended that anyone would say otherwise. She followed up *Uncle Tom's Cabin* with an 1853 book titled *The Key to Uncle Tom's Cabin*. In this second book, she detailed large numbers of documents and testimonials from eyewitnesses proving stories such as the ones she told in *Uncle Tom's*

Harriet Beecher Stowe took particular offense at criticism of Uncle Tom's Cabin *because of all the work she put into it. She said she wrote it "with her heart's blood. Many times ... I thought my health would fail utterly; but I prayed earnestly that God would help me till I got through, and still I am pressed beyond measure and above strength."*

An illustration from an early edition of Uncle Tom's Cabin

Cabin did happen.

Stowe became hated by most Southerners. She was seen as someone who was trying to destroy the Southern way of life. It became dangerous in the South to admit owning or reading a copy of *Uncle Tom's Cabin.* Children in Richmond, Virginia, even had a sidewalk chant that was popular at the time: "Go, go, go, Ol' Harriet Beecher Stowe! We don't want you here in Virginny. Go, go, go!"

Stowe began to get threatening letters from people living in the South. Finally, she quit reading hate letters and answered only the positive ones.

One day a package came to the house that the Stowes couldn't ignore. Calvin opened the package and discovered it contained the ear of a slave. The sender warned this was what could happen to slaves if Stowe continued her crusade against slavery. ❧

Harriet Beecher Stowe

6 ACCLAIM IN EUROPE

❧⨳☙

Calvin decided to take a job he had been offered teaching at a seminary in Andover, Massachusetts. Even though she was now a famous author, Harriet continued to see herself as a wife and mother first and foremost. She immediately set to work making a home for her family in the new community.

Harriet didn't like the house the Stowes first were offered. She asked if the seminary would allow them to convert an old gymnasium into their home. Seminary officials said they didn't mind.

Stowe used some of the money she earned from her book to make the gymnasium usable. The Stowes lived in a boardinghouse until the gym was ready.

Then an exciting new prospect arose. For as hated as Stowe was in the South, she was adored in

A freedwoman from Philadelphia reads Uncle Tom's Cabin *at a gathering in London, England, in 1856.*

> *The gymnasium the Stowes converted into their home had once been the place where seminary students made coffins. Students made the famous Andover coffins to help pay for their education.*

Europe. In Scotland, the Glasgow Ladies' Anti-Slavery Society and the Glasgow Female New Association for the Abolition of Slavery invited Stowe to star in a speaking tour of England and Scotland. The groups would pay her expenses, as well as Calvin's. She readily agreed.

Harriet, Calvin, and Harriet's brother Charles left from New York in April 1853 and arrived in Liverpool, England, 10 days later. The group sailed on one of the newest vessels, a clipper ship, so named for the way it "clipped off" the miles in a speedy fashion. Stowe was worried she would be seasick, but she wasn't. In fact, she loved the excitement of her journey.

Making her first trip overseas, Stowe was shocked at the reactions she got. *Uncle Tom's Cabin* was wildly popular in Europe. One and a half million copies of the book had been sold in England in the first year. People waited for hours just to get a glimpse of its 41-year-old author. Huge crowds waited for her at railroad stations, and children brought her bouquets of flowers. Songs were composed in her honor. Harriet wasn't used to all the sudden attention and was a little overwhelmed.

"Nobody expected anything, nobody said anything, and so I wrote freely," Stowe said about writing

Harriet and Calvin Stowe in the early 1850s

Uncle Tom's Cabin. "Now what embarrasses me is to be announced as an attraction—to have eyes fixed on me and people all waiting."

Stowe had never spoken in front of large audiences and wasn't really excited to do so. Calvin Stowe was used to giving lectures, so he ended up doing most of the speaking on the tour. The crowds weren't disappointed, though. Harriet shook hands and chatted

> *Stowe felt a little over-*
> *whelmed by all the*
> *attention she received*
> *in England and looked*
> *forward to blending in*
> *more in other foreign*
> *countries she visited.*
> *Some of her favorite*
> *memories from her trip*
> *included hiking*
> *Alpine trails with her*
> *brother Charles and*
> *painting pictures of*
> *flowers and mountains.*

with people who wanted to meet her. That was enough for her adoring fans.

In all, Stowe spent five months in Europe. She stayed in London for several weeks before leaving to tour France, Switzerland, Germany, and Belgium. She met lords and ladies and popular authors who accepted her as their equal. Many times, Stowe met famous people but didn't realize it.

"I am always finding out, a day or two after, that I have been with somebody very remarkable, and did not know it at the time," she wrote.

Along with meeting countless people, Stowe saw the sights. She visited churches and museums. She even became a work of art herself. Though it took a great deal of talking to convince her, Stowe agreed to have her picture painted by George Richmond, one of the most famous portrait painters of the time.

"If people really knew me they wouldn't make such a fuss over me," Stowe told him.

Stowe also collected money and gifts for the antislavery movement, as well as personal tokens. One of her most treasured gifts was a collection of 26 leather-bound books. They were filled with the signatures of women from throughout the British Empire, asking the women of the United States to bring slavery to an end. All totaled, 562,448 women had signed the books. The books made Stowe feel even better about the work she was doing—and they would come in handy at a very important time in American history. ❧

An engraving from an original drawing by artist George Richmond, who painted Stowe's portrait in 1853

7 A DIFFERENT LIFE

❧

In September 1853, Stowe took the steamer *Arctic* back home to Andover, Massachusetts, from England. Money she was earning from her writing made life easier. She had been able to hire a full-time cook and a maid. A woman also came to the Stowe household twice a week to do the laundry and mend clothing, tasks Stowe had always hated.

Stowe had needed the help before, but it was even more necessary now. She received so much mail each day that it was delivered in a special sack. Among the letters were hundreds of offers to speak at various events. Too shy to speak publicly and because of the social constraints of the time that discouraged women from speaking in public, Stowe politely declined the offers. But she did write speeches

Harriet Beecher Stowe posed for a studio portrait in the mid-1800s.

Stowe had always been generous with her money, but she never spent much on herself. Late in her life, her daughters said they could never remember their mother owning more than four or five dresses at one time. Stowe also refused to buy a carriage and a team of horses. She said she couldn't afford the upkeep.

for other people to deliver.

In addition to writing speeches, Stowe wrote about one magazine article every two weeks attacking slavery in the last months of 1853 and all of 1854. At the same time, the Stowe home was becoming a gathering place for antislavery activities. Among their guests were abolitionist William Lloyd Garrison, Frederick Douglass, a former fugitive slave who now was working to free all slaves, and Sojourner Truth, a former slave who spoke out against slavery.

By 1860, Stowe's writing had put her at the top of her field. She had more readers than any other U.S. writer, and her income was higher than any other author. Between 1856 and 1860, Stowe earned about $6,000 each month, an enormous amount of money when, for example, a loaf of bread cost a penny.

In 1856, Stowe decided to return to Europe. This time, she went with Calvin, her twin daughters, Eliza and Hattie, her son Henry, and her sister Mary. The group left from New York on a steamer in June and arrived in Liverpool, England, in mid-July.

When it was time to leave England, Calvin returned to his job in the United States, and Henry

135,000 SETS, 270,000 VOLUMES SOLD.

UNCLE TOM'S CABIN

FOR SALE HERE.

AN EDITION FOR THE MILLION, COMPLETE IN 1 Vol., PRICE 37 1-2 CENTS.
    "   "   IN GERMAN, IN 1 Vol., PRICE 50 CENTS.
    "   "   IN 2 Vols,. CLOTH, 6 PLATES, PRICE $1.50.
SUPERB ILLUSTRATED EDITION, IN 1 Vol., WITH 153 ENGRAVINGS,
PRICES FROM $2.50 TO $5.00.

The Greatest Book of the Age.

went back to begin college. Harriet, Mary, and the twins went on to Paris, France, one of Harriet's favorite places in the world. While there, Stowe visited a school where she accepted a donation collected by

Uncle Tom's Cabin and other writings made Harriet Beecher Stowe a wealthy woman.

Harriet and her twin daughters, Harriet (Hattie) and Eliza. The twins never married and lived with their parents. As adults, they managed the family home in Hartford.

children who had read *Uncle Tom's Cabin*. They wanted the money to be used to help fight slavery.

Eliza and Hattie would stay in Paris for two years and go to school. Harriet and Mary headed to

Italy on February 1, 1857. Still loving adventure, 45-year-old Stowe visited Pompeii and climbed Mount Vesuvius.

The women headed back to England when an invitation to visit arrived from Anne Isabella Milbanke, the widow of Lord Byron, Harriet's favorite poet. Lady Byron and Stowe had met on an earlier trip and had grown to be close friends. Lady Byron was sick in bed when they arrived, but she was happy to see Stowe. They got together two more times before Harriet and Mary headed back to the United States that summer.

Harriet and Mary faced many difficulties on their way to Rome, Italy. At one point, they were riding in a carriage in which the wheels fell off twice! The driver also kept demanding more money from them to continue the journey. In addition, a mob surrounded the carriage at one point asking for money. Later in the trip, Harriet and Mary feared their luggage might be stolen. However, they and their luggage arrived safely.

While Lady Byron recovered from her illness, Stowe couldn't shake the feeling of death from her mind. Even as the ship moved across the Atlantic carrying her home, Harriet knew something bad was about to happen.

Chapter

8 THE CIVIL WAR

❧❧❧

Back in the United States at the end of June 1857, Stowe found all was well—though it wouldn't be for long. On July 9, her son Henry drowned while swimming in the Connecticut River in New Hampshire. He had just finished his freshman year at Dartmouth College.

Stowe was devastated, and she spiraled into despair. Henry had died without having a religious conversion experience. Everything in Stowe's faith and upbringing taught her that her son was now damned to hell. She wrote *The Minister's Wooing* as a way to process her grief and come to terms with her own evolving faith. After the book was published, she returned to her antislavery work.

By the late 1850s, the North and South were growing more divided despite President James Buchanan's efforts to keep them together. Buchanan personally opposed slavery, but believed the Constitution protected it.

In 1860, a tall, lanky man from Illinois named Abraham Lincoln was elected president of the United States. At his inauguration in 1861, Lincoln stated his presidential position on slavery. It didn't differ a great deal from Buchanan's beliefs.

"I have no purpose, directly or indirectly to interfere with the institution of slavery in the states where it exists," he said. "I believe I have no lawful right to do so, and I have no inclination to do so."

While Lincoln said he would not interfere with slavery, personally he hated it. "If slavery is not wrong, nothing is wrong," he once said. However as president, Lincoln was looking at the bigger picture. He was trying to hold the Union together.

Southerners didn't believe Lincoln would allow slavery to continue, even to keep the country united. Before the presidential election, Southern leaders had agreed that the South should secede from the United States if Lincoln were elected.

In December 1860, South Carolina became the first state to withdraw from the Union. In January 1861, Alabama, Florida, Georgia, Louisiana, and Mississippi followed South Carolina's lead. Texas seceded in February. Leaders from these states met in Montgomery, Alabama, to set up the Confederate

An 1861 engraving shows the bombardment of Fort Sumter on April 12.

States of America. They elected Jefferson Davis president and Alexander Stephens vice president.

Buchanan, who remained president until March, did nothing, hoping these states would tire of being separate and eventually rejoin the Union. In time, four more states would secede—Virginia, North Carolina, Arkansas, and Tennessee.

Lincoln, too, hoped the United States still could be saved. However, he would not stand idly by. Though he didn't want a war, Lincoln warned Southerners he would use whatever power was necessary to hold on to the country's federally owned property in the South. When the Confederates fired on Fort Sumter in Charleston, South Carolina, on April 12, 1861, the president held true to his word.

The Civil War had begun.

Along with most others in the North, Stowe thought the war would end quickly with a Northern victory. Meanwhile, Southerners believed they would quickly be victorious. After all, they were fighting for their way of life.

Harriet and Calvin's son Frederick yearned to join the troops fighting for the North's cause. Stowe feared Frederick wasn't strong enough to fight and would end up getting sick.

Stowe wrote to one of her daughters at the beginning of the war:

> *Ever since war was declared which is now about two weeks—a little over—I have been like a person struggling in a nightmare dream. Fred immediately wanted to go, and I was willing he should if he could only get a situation where he could do any good. ... Fred and I had a long talk Sunday night and he said he was willing to lay down his life for the cause and that if he died he felt he should go to the pure and good he had always longed for, and he and I kneeled down hand in hand and prayed for each other.*

Frederick would be honored for his bravery in action, but Stowe continued to worry about him. In the summer of 1863, Stowe's fears came true. Frederick went into battle and was wounded at Gettysburg, Pennsylvania. A chaplain wrote to the Stowes to tell them of Frederick's injuries:

> *It may cheer your heart to know that he is in the hands of good, kind friends. He was struck by a fragment of a shell, which entered his right ear. He is quiet and cheerful, longs to see some member of his family, and is, above all, anxious that they should hear from him as soon as possible.*

Harriet and Calvin visited Frederick in a New York military hospital in November. Frederick stayed in the hospital for three months because the wound wouldn't heal properly. Then, unfit for further military service, Frederick was honorably

The casulties were enormous on both sides at the Battle of Gettysburg.

discharged from service and went home where his parents could care for him.

The fun-loving boy who had been full of life came home a different person. Frederick had lost the hearing in one ear. He also suffered from terrible headaches. His nerves shattered, and struggling with alcoholism and morphine addiction, Frederick was never himself again.

Frederick Stowe's alcoholism became much worse after he was wounded at Gettysburg.

Though Stowe had hoped war could be avoided, she believed Lincoln would eventually free the slaves. However, she wasn't pleased with how slow the change was to come about. She also was angry when Lincoln said his first priority was to save the Union, not to destroy slavery.

Stowe became even angrier when Lincoln removed John Charles Frémont from his command of the Union Army's Western Department early in the Civil War. On his own, Frémont had decided to take over the property of Missouri slave owners. He also planned to free all their slaves, a bold move that Stowe applauded. Lincoln, on the other hand, was angered by Frémont's actions and transferred him to western Virginia.

With Harriet's encouragement, Calvin wrote to their old friend Salmon Chase, who now was serving as Lincoln's treasury secretary. He wrote:

> *I do not know that you have either the time or inclination to listen to a word from the common people, but I wish you could hear the cries of surprise, indignation, disgust and contempt, which now everywhere find utterance at the removal of Frémont.*

Others questioned the president as well, including Horace Greeley, the editor of the *New York Tribune*. In a letter to Greeley, Lincoln tried to explain his actions.

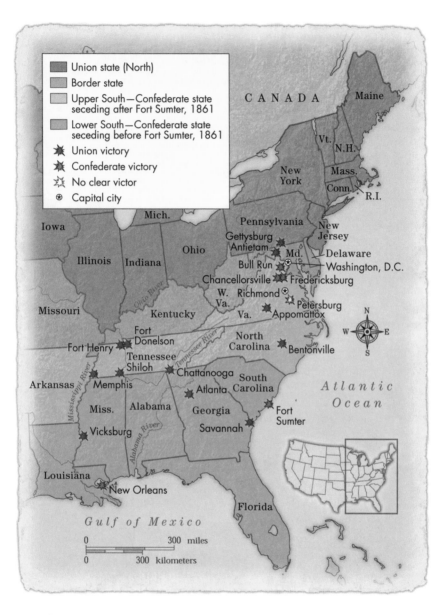

Union state (North)
Border state
Upper South—Confederate state seceding after Fort Sumter, 1861
Lower South—Confederate state seceding before Fort Sumter, 1861
✴ Union victory
✴ Confederate victory
✴ No clear victor
⊗ Capital city

C A N A D A

Maine

Vt.
N.H.
Mass.
Conn.
R.I.

New York
New Jersey
Delaware
Washington, D.C.

Iowa
Mich.
Pennsylvania
Gettysburg
Antietam
Md.
Bull Run
Chancellorsville
Fredericksburg
W. Va.
Richmond
Petersburg
Appomattox

Illinois
Indiana
Ohio

Missouri
Kentucky
Va.

Fort Donelson
Fort Henry
Tennessee
Shiloh
Chattanooga
North Carolina
Bentonville

Arkansas
Memphis
South Carolina

Miss.
Alabama
Atlanta
Georgia
Savannah
Fort Sumter

Vicksburg

Louisiana
New Orleans

Florida

Atlantic Ocean

N
W   E
S

Gulf of Mexico

0   300 miles
0   300 kilometers

Major battles of the Civil War were fought in the North and the South.

"My paramount object in this struggle is to save the Union and is not to save or destroy slavery," Lincoln wrote. "If I could save the Union without freeing any slave, I would do it; and if I could save it by freeing all the slaves, I would do it; and if I could do it by freeing some and leaving others alone, I would also do that."

While Stowe didn't want to see the Union divided, in her eyes the Civil War was simply a fight about slavery. Freeing the slaves was even more important than saving the Union. Why had she allowed her son Frederick to join the fighting if not to free the slaves? Stowe didn't see slavery as one piece in a larger puzzle. It was the only piece. While the slavery issue always remained the top priority in her mind, Stowe would come to see the bigger picture when she met Lincoln in 1862. She wrote:

> *I am going to Washington to see the heads of Department myself and to satisfy myself that I may refer to the Emancipation Proclamation as a reality and a substance not to fizzle out of the little end of the horn.*

In the Emancipation Proclamation, President Lincoln announced African-American troops would help the Union. About 180,000 blacks fought as part of the Union Army. About 120,000 of them were slaves who had fled to the North in search of freedom. Many abolitionists thought the Emancipation Proclamation had not gone far enough because it only freed slaves in Confederate states. Slaves in border states would not be freed. Abolitionists stepped up work on a constitutional amendment to end slavery. The 13th Amendment was ratified in June 1865.

hinted it likely would follow along with whatever Great Britain did.

Before Stowe could safely write an article calling on British women to speak out against the Confederacy, she wanted to be certain Lincoln was serious about freeing the slaves. Then she could use this in her article.

Mary Todd Lincoln, the president's wife, made arrangements for Stowe to meet her husband at a tea at the White House. Massachusetts Senator Henry Wilson and his wife were also invited. When Lincoln met Stowe, he smiled and called her "the little lady who wrote the book that started this great war." Although today, "great" means wonderful, in Stowe's time the word referred to size and more accurately meant "huge."

On January 1, 1863, Lincoln issued the Emancipation Proclamation. It freed all the slaves in the states that had seceded from the Union. That day, Calvin and Harriet were in Boston attending a concert at the Boston Music Hall. When the crowd realized Stowe was there, they chanted her name until she stood in silent acceptance of the honor.

Stowe's article ran in the January issue of *The Atlantic Monthly* magazine as planned. She wrote about the meaning of the Emancipation Proclamation and scolded the British women for supporting the South, reminding them of their former stand against slavery.

The first reading of the 1863 Emancipation Proclamation by President Lincoln and his Cabinet

We appeal to you as sisters, as wives, as mothers, to raise your voices to your fellow citizens, and your prayers to God for the removal of this affliction and disgrace from the Christian world.

Meanwhile, her brother Henry conducted a speaking tour in Great Britain to rally support for the North and the antislavery cause. He often used words taken from Harriet's antislavery articles.

Great Britain never recognized the Confederacy. Lincoln later said he believed this was because of *Uncle Tom's Cabin*, Harriet's article in *The Atlantic Monthly*, and Henry Ward Beecher's speaking tour in Great Britain. ✒

9 REBUILDING THE SOUTH

Chapter

◦⟨×⟩◦

The Civil War dragged on until 1865 when, on April 9, Confederate Genderal Robert E. Lee surrendered to Union General Ullysses S. Grant at Virginia's Appomattox Court House.

Six days later, President Abraham Lincoln died from an assassin's bullet. After the war's end, great tension remained between the North and the South. Many Northerners wanted revenge for Lincoln's death as well as all the lives lost in the Civil War. Yet, before his death, Lincoln urged the entire country to heal its wounds and move forward as one. Though anger between the North and South continued for years, no large outbreaks of violence occurred.

At the end of the war, two big questions remained. How should the once divided country be reunited, and

Richmond, Virginia, and other Southern cities were in ruins after the Civil War.

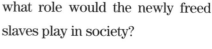

> *About 620,000 soldiers died in the Civil War. Disease caused more than half the deaths.*

what role would the newly freed slaves play in society?

The Civil War had left the South shattered. Several of its largest cities were destroyed. Southern ports and the railroad system had been ruined. Leaders in the North and South had to find a way to rebuild the South. They also had to agree on how the 11 states that had seceded from the Union would rejoin the country.

After Lincoln's assassination, Vice President Andrew Johnson became president. Harriet supported Johnson's plan for Reconstruction of the South. He said all Southern white people should be pardoned. The Southern states would form new state governments that had to abolish slavery. Officials of the new governments also had to swear loyalty to the United States. Once a state completed these steps, it would be allowed back in the Union. By 1870, all of the states had rejoined the Union.

Stowe believed Johnson's plan was fair. She was among the first to say she favored compassion for the South after it rejoined the Union. She felt defeat and the end of slavery were punishment enough for the South. "One nation must live in brotherhood," she wrote.

Stowe traveled to the South several times after the Civil War ended and was saddened to see all the

Harriet Beecher Stowe said the South should not be punished further after the Civil War.

destruction. She wrote to a friend:

> *I wish you could know of the sorrow and suffering I see, among people that one cannot help pitying. Yet a brighter day is breaking for both white and black.*

On one trip, Stowe visited the Confederate war memorial in Savannah, Georgia. She had always hoped the country could reach a peaceful end to slavery. Her heart was heavy with the thought that so many people lost their lives in a long, bloody war. She also felt that such sorrow was the price God exacted from a country—North and South—that had ignored for so long the grief of slave mothers mourning for their lost children.

Slavery was officially ended when the United States ratified the 13th Amendment to the Constitution in 1865. Yet, Stowe knew her work was not done. She realized freed blacks would face a difficult road ahead, and she was determined to do what she could to help them.

She also tried to help her son Frederick get back on his feet. Though still hated in the South, Stowe invested in an old cotton plantation in Florida called Laurel Grove. Frederick would help manage the plantation, and Harriet and Calvin would join him in the winter months. The plantation served as more than just something for Frederick to do. It provided jobs for more than 100 former slaves.

After two years, Stowe realized the plantation was costing too much to run. Frederick failed as a manager, and the plantation was losing money each month.

In 1867, Stowe bought a 200-acre (80-hectare) orange grove in Mandarin, Florida. She hoped that Frederick would be better suited—and happier—working there. He wasn't. However, Stowe did take the opportunity to open a school for former slaves in the community.

Stowe loved Florida. In 1873, she published *Palmetto Leaves*, a collection of sketches and essays about the state. The book became a best seller, and readers wanted to see what Stowe so loved about Florida. By the following year, land was in such demand in the Mandarin area, real estate prices doubled.

Harriet (second from right) sits next to husband Calvin and four other people at their home in Mandarin, Florida.

Florida newspapers gave Stowe credit for turning Florida into a winter getaway for Northerners. Soon, railroads offered expanded services to Florida from Northern cities in the winter months. Stowe had helped jump-start the tourist industry in Florida.

Southerners watched Stowe and the work she did. Among those watching her was former Confederate general Robert E. Lee, who liked what Stowe was doing and publicly said so. Gradually, Southerners came to accept her. ꙮ

10 THE FINAL YEARS

❧❧❧

Through her entire life, Stowe would rather listen to others than talk. However, at age 61 Stowe agreed to go on a speaking tour and give lectures on her books. She had never really given public speeches to audiences of men and women before, but once again she needed the money.

In 1872, Stowe toured New England and read passages from some of her best-loved books. Her lectures sold out everywhere she went.

Stowe traveled from city to city by train. The food was bad, and the hotels she stayed in were dreary. Yet, she came to love life on the lecture circuit.

"I never sleep better than after a long day's ride," she said.

At first, Stowe was shy about speaking in front

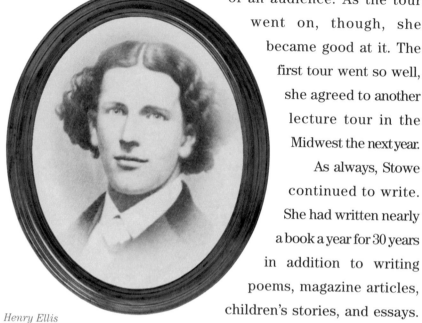

Henry Ellis Stowe had drowned while swimming in New Hampshire.

of an audience. As the tour went on, though, she became good at it. The first tour went so well, she agreed to another lecture tour in the Midwest the next year.

As always, Stowe continued to write. She had written nearly a book a year for 30 years in addition to writing poems, magazine articles, children's stories, and essays. None of these other writings, though, would equal the success of *Uncle Tom's Cabin*.

Keeping busy helped Stowe hide from the pain in her heart over her sons Samuel Charles, who died as a baby, Henry Ellis, who drowned in 1857, and Frederick, who in 1870 went to California and disappeared. She never heard from Frederick again, though for the rest of her life she kept thinking he would return.

Despite the pain that remained, Stowe knew she had been very fortunate. She also knew she had made a difference. In Florida, Stowe saw black men become educated and buy property. The greatest event in her life, she said, was the abolition of slavery.

Stowe wrote:

> *An old Negro friend in our neighborhood has got a new, nice two-story house, and an orange grove, and a sugar mill. He has got a lot of money besides. Mr. Stowe met him one day, and he said, 'I have got 20 head of cattle, four head of 'hoss,' 40 head of hen, and I have got 10 children, all mine, every one mine.' Well, now, that is a thing that a black man could not say once, and this man was 60 years old before he could say it.*

Stowe, too, bloomed later in her life. She had become an international celebrity. Her circle of friends grew to include famous authors, including Mark Twain and Oliver Wendell Holmes, as well as nobility in Europe. Yet Stowe never really changed. She remained a plain, modest person who thought herself no better than anyone else.

Stowe was active and involved in Hartford events.

Harriet Beecher Stowe lived to be 85 years old.

The Stowe house in Hartford, Connecticut, was built in 1871.

She helped revitalize the local art museum and started an art school that eventually became the University of Hartford. She dabbled in oil painting, which she had taught herself when she was in her 60s, and she

published her last book, *Poganuc People*, in 1878.

As the years went by, Harriet's love for Calvin deepened. They worried less about money because their daughters took over managing the household. Calvin started seeing his phantoms more often the older he became, but his mind otherwise stayed sharp. A great companion to her husband, Stowe was at his bedside when he died on August 22, 1886, at age 85.

During her later years, Stowe may have had a series of strokes. Her mind began to wander more and more. She spent her time looking at picture books, picking flowers, and taking long walks with her nurse. On good days when her mind was clear, Harriet talked about *Uncle Tom's Cabin*.

Just before midnight on July 1, 1896, Harriet Beecher Stowe quietly died at age 85. She was buried between her husband, Calvin, and their son Henry in the Andover Chapel Cemetery in Andover, Massachusetts.

Beautiful bouquets of flowers stood along the sides of Stowe's grave. On top of her casket lay a very special wreath. The card accompanying the wreath said: "The Children of Uncle Tom." 🍂

> *Even as an old woman, Stowe remained a bit of a tomboy for her day. Long after her own children were grown up, Stowe asked a little girl she saw on the street to teach her to ride a bike.*

STOWE'S LIFE

1811

Harriet Elizabeth
Beecher is born
June 14 in Litchfield,
Connecticut

1816

Roxanna, Harriet's
mother, dies

1832

Beecher family moves
to Cincinnati, Ohio

1810

1830

1809

Louis Braille of
France, inventor of a
writing system for the
blind, is born

1821

Central American
countries gain
independence
from Spain

1833

Great Britain
abolishes slavery

WORLD EVENTS

1836
Marries Calvin Ellis
Stowe on January 6

1845
Falls ill with cholera
during a summer
outbreak and
nearly dies

1846
Recovers her health
after visiting a spa in
Brattleboro, Vermont

1845

1836
Texans defeat
Mexican troops
at San Jacinto after
a deadly battle at
the Alamo

1846
Irish potato famine
reaches its worst

STOWE'S LIFE

1851

Uncle Tom's Cabin is printed in the *National Era* beginning June 5

1850

The Stowes move to Maine where Harriet writes *Uncle Tom's Cabin*

1849

The Stowes' infant son Charley dies of cholera

1850

1848

The Communist Manifesto by German writer Karl Marx is widely distributed

1850

Jeans are invented by Levi Strauss, a German who moved to California during the gold rush.

WORLD EVENTS

1853

Makes first trip to
Europe; *The Key to
Uncle Tom's Cabin*
is published to back
up materials found in
Stowe's first book

1852

Uncle Tom's Cabin is
published in book
form in March, a
month before the seri-
alized version is fin-
ished in the *National
Era;* the Stowes move
to Andover,
Massachusetts

1856

Returns
to Europe

1855

1852

Postage stamps are
widely used

1858

English scientist
Charles Darwin
presents his theory
of evolution

STOWE'S LIFE

1868

Buys an orange grove in Florida

1863

On January 1, President Abraham Lincoln issues the Emancipation Proclamation; shortly after, Stowe publishes an article asking British women to make sure Great Britain doesn't recognize the Confederacy

1872

Reads passages from her books during a lecture tour of New England

1865

1865

Lewis Carroll writes *Alice's Adventures in Wonderland*

1869

The periodic table of elements is invented by Dimitri Mendeleyev

1860

Austrian composer Gustav Mahler is born in Kalischt (now in Austria)

WORLD EVENTS

1886

Calvin dies on
August 6

1873

Palmetto Leaves is
published and helps
make Florida a
popular destination
for travelers

1896

Dies on July 1 in
Hartford, Connecticut

1885

1882

Thomas Edison
builds a power
station

1886

Grover Cleveland
dedicates the Statue
of Liberty in New
York, a gift from the
people of France

1893

Women gain voting
privileges in New
Zealand, the first
country to take such
a step

NICKNAME: Hattie

DATE OF BIRTH: June 14, 1811

BIRTHPLACE: Litchfield, Connecticut

FATHER: Lyman Beecher
(1775–1863)

MOTHER: Roxanna Foote Beecher
(1775–1816)

EDUCATION: Attended Litchfield
Academy and Hartford
Female Seminary

SPOUSE: Calvin Ellis Stowe
1802–1886

DATE OF MARRIAGE: January 6, 1836

CHILDREN: Harriet (1836–1907)
Eliza (1836–1912)
Henry (1838–1857)
Frederick (1840–presumed
dead 1870)
Georgianna (1843–1890)
Samuel Charles (1848–1849)
Charles Edward
(1850–1934)

DATE OF DEATH: July 1, 1896

PLACE OF BURIAL: Andover, Massachusetts

In the Library

Bloom, Harold. *Harriet Beecher Stowe's Uncle Tom's Cabin.* New York: Chelsea House Publishers, 1996.

Fritz, Jean. *Harriet Beecher Stowe and the Beecher Preachers.* New York: G. P. Putnam's Sons, 1994.

Gelletly, Leeanne. *Harriet Beecher Stowe: Author of Uncle Tom's Cabin.* Philadelphia: Chelsea House, 2000.

Heinrichs, Ann. *The Emancipation Proclamation.* Minneapolis: Compass Point Books, 2002.

Stanchak, John E. *Civil War.* New York: Dorling Kindersley, 2000.

ON THE WEB

For more information on *Harriet Beecher Stowe*, use FactHound to track down Web sites related to this book.

1. Go to *www.facthound.com*
2. Type in a search word related to this book or this book ID: 0756508223
3. Click on the *Fetch It* button.

FactHound will find the best Web sites for you.

HISTORIC SITES

Harriet Beecher Stowe Center
77 Forest St.
Hartford, CT 06105
860/522-9258
To see Harriet Beecher Stowe's Hartford home and visit a museum and library devoted to her

Harriet Beecher Stowe House
2950 Gilbert Ave.
State Route 3, U.S. 22
Cincinnati, OH 45214
513/632-5100
To see the Cincinnati home where Harriet Beecher Stowe lived with her father and siblings and to learn more about black history

abolitionists
people who supported the banning of slavery

cholera
an acute diarrheal disease caused by too much bacteria in the small intestine

fiancé
the man a woman is engaged to marry

installments
parts of a story that are issued separately

philosophy
the study of truth, wisdom, and reality

radical
favoring extreme changes or reforms

Reconstruction
the system for bringing the Southern states back into the United States after the Civil War

royalty
a payment to an author for each copy of a book sold

secede
withdraw from

serial
a story in a magazine or newspaper that continues for more than one issue

spindle
a rod around which something is turned

steamer
a ship powered by steam

tuberculosis
a contagious disease that usually affects a person's lungs

Chapter 1

Page 11, line 8: Joan D. Hedrick. *Harriet Beecher Stowe: A Life.* New York: Oxford University Press, 1994, p. 207.

Chapter 2

Page 15, line 1: Johanna Johnston. *Runaway to Heaven: The Story of Harriet Beecher Stowe and Her Era.* Garden City, N.Y.: Doubleday, 1963, p. 5.

Page 16, line 24: Edward Wagenknecht. *Harriet Beecher Stowe: The Known and the Unknown.* New York: Oxford University Press, 1965, p. 22.

Page 20, line 14: Noel B. Gerson. *Harriet Beecher Stowe.* New York: Praeger Publishers, 1976, p. 6.

Chapter 3

Page 31, line 26: *Harriet Beecher Stowe: A Life*, p. 136.

Page 35, line 6: *Harriet Beecher Stowe: The Known and the Unknown*, p. 93.

Chapter 4

Page 37, line 5: *Runaway to Heaven: The Story of Harriet Beecher Stowe and Her Era*, p. 176.

Page 41, line 18: Ibid., p. 203.

Page 42, line 2: Ibid., p. 204.

Page 45, line 4: *Harriet Beecher Stowe: The Known and the Unknown*, p. 183.

Page 46, line 11: *Runaway to Heaven: The Story of Harriet Beecher Stowe and Her Era*, p. 203.

Chapter 5

Page 57, line 3: Ibid., p. 263.

Chapter 6

Page 60, line 27: *Harriet Beecher Stowe: The Known and the Unknown*, p. 166.

Page 62, line 13: *Harriet Beecher Stowe*, p. 94.

Page 62, line 23: Ibid., p. 89.

Chapter 7

Page 69, line 19: *Harriet Beecher Stowe*, p. 126.

Chapter 8

Page 72, line 9: *Runaway to Heaven: The Story of Harriet Beecher Stowe and Her Era*, p. 345.

Page 74, line 16: *Harriet Beecher Stowe: The Known and the Unknown*, p. 67.

Page 75, line 6: *Runaway to Heaven: The Story of Harriet Beecher Stowe and Her Era*, p. 364.

Page 77, line 19: Ibid., p. 351.

Page 78, line 1: Ibid., p. 354.

Page 79, line 21: Ibid., p. 356.

Page 82, line 12: *Harriet Beecher Stowe: A Life*, p. vii.

Page 83, line 1: *Runaway to Heaven: The Story of Harriet Beecher Stowe and Her Era*, p. 358.

Chapter 9

Page 86, line 25: *Harriet Beecher Stowe*, p. 175.

Page 87, line 2: *Runaway to Heaven: The Story of Harriet Beecher Stowe and Her Era*, p. 389.

Chapter 10

Page 91, line 13: David McCullough. *Brave Companions: Portraits in History.* New York: Prentice Hall Press, 1992, p. 50.

Page 93, line 2: *Harriet Beecher Stowe*, p. 207.

Adams, John R. *Harriet Beecher Stowe.* New York: Twayne Publishers, 1963.

Downs, Robert B., et al. *Memorable Americans: 1750-1950.* Littleton, Colo.: Libraries Unlimited, 1983.

Gerson, Noel B. *Harriet Beecher Stowe.* New York: Praeger Publishers, 1976.

Hedrick, Joan D. *Harriet Beecher Stowe: A Life.* New York: Oxford University Press, 1994.

Hillstrom, Kevin, and Laurie Collier Hillstrom. *American Civil War Almanac.* Detroit: UXL, 2000.

Hillstrom, Kevin, and Laurie Collier Hillstrom. *American Civil War Biographies. Vol. I-II.* Detroit: UXL, 2000.

Johnston, Johanna. *Runaway to Heaven: The Story of Harriet Beecher Stowe and Her Era.* Garden City, N.Y.: Doubleday, 1963.

McCullough, David. *Brave Companions: Portraits in History.* New York: Prentice Hall Press, 1992.

McHenry, Robert. *Famous Americans.* New York: Dover, 1980.

Stoddard, Hope. *Famous American Women.* New York: Crowell, 1970.

Stowe, Charles Edward, and Lyman Beecher Stowe. *Harriet Beecher Stowe: The Story of Her Life.* Boston: Houghton Mifflin, 1911.

Stowe, Harriet Beecher. *Uncle Tom's Cabin.* London: Piper Brothers and Co., 1852.

Wagenknecht, Edward. *Harriet Beecher Stowe: The Known and the Unknown.* New York: Oxford University Press, 1965.

White, Hilda. *Truth Is My Country: Portraits of Eight New England Authors.* New York: Doubleday, 1971.

Brenda Haugen is the author and editor of many books, most of them for children. A graduate of the University of North Dakota in Grand Forks, Brenda lives in North Dakota with her family.

Image Credits